Garden of Youth

Setty T

Garden of Youth © 2024 Setty T

All rights reserved.

No part of this publication may be reproduced, stored in a retrieval system, or transmitted, in any form or by any means, electronic, mechanical, photocopying, recording or otherwise, without the prior written permission of the presenters.

Setty T asserts the moral right to be identified as author of this work.

Presentation by *BookLeaf Publishing*

Web: www.bookleafpub.com

E-mail: info@bookleafpub.com

ISBN: 9789363310759

First edition 2024

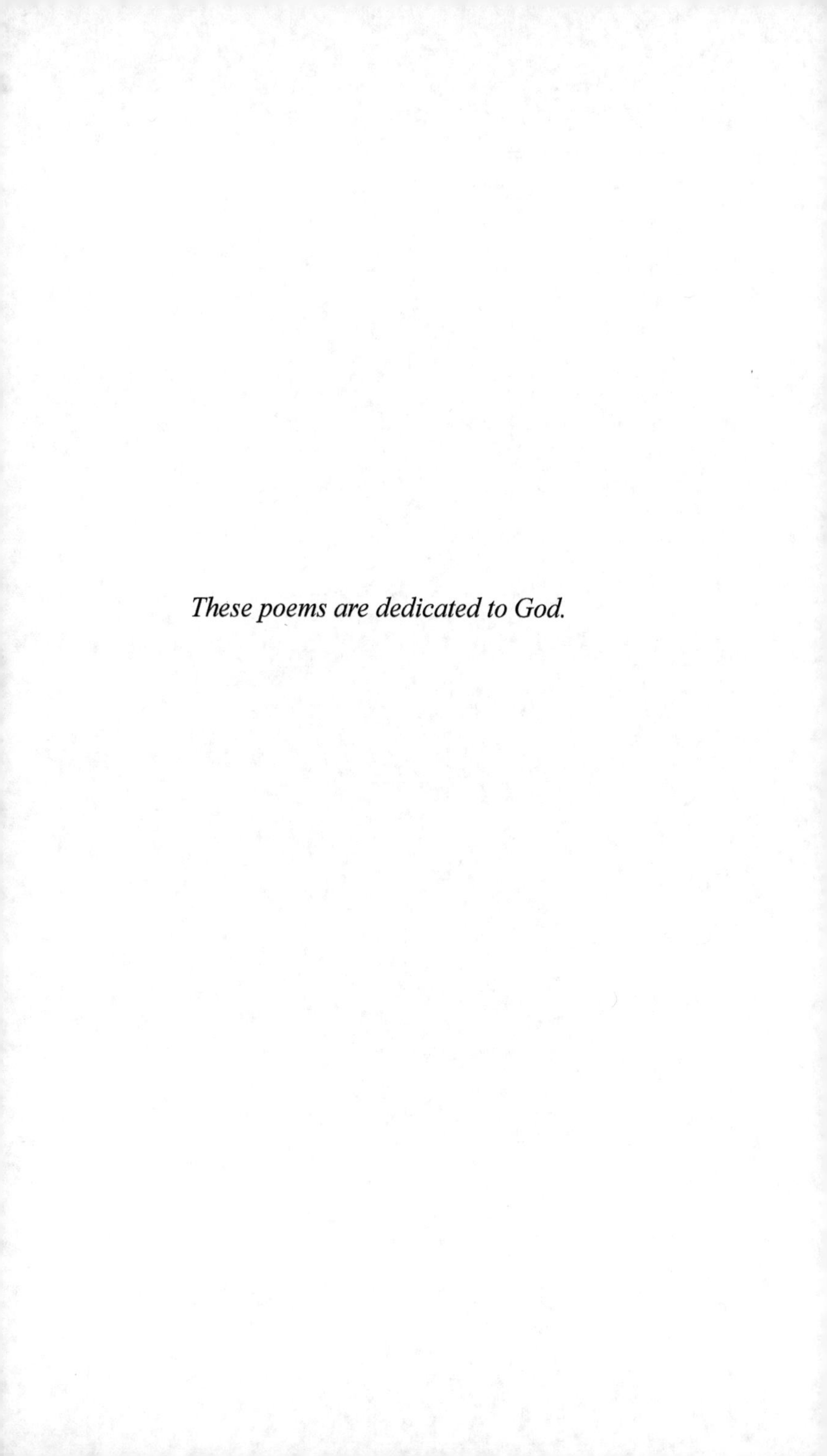

These poems are dedicated to God.

PREFACE

The world destroys and rebuilds itself every day. It does so through phones, computers, television, and so much more. The media people engage with is designed to be fast, to be marketable, to be consumed for a second and then spit out. It is so easy to feel pointless in a world that cannot decide on a point to stay at. As I grew in this whirlwind of a time, I would ground myself with decisive words. I would do my best to, when I was anxious or stressed, write something. God gave me words to be an anchor for my thoughts and writing to be the ship that sailed them into poetry. I wish to share my reflections in those off moments with you, and hopefully encourage you to think. I want you to feel how I felt, through the highs and the lows of my eighteen years on this earth. I hope you enjoy what I have put together, and that your worldview grows wider after reading.

With The Stars

Maybe if I stay out here long
all my pain will be gone.
I can see the starry sky
drift into morning, say goodbye.
I'll wonder in the damp grass,
when did everything go so fast?
And to the last star of the night
I'll make a wish, shining bright.
I hope soon you'll take me away
make me feel as I did that day.
As a child, eyes bright
like a star in the night.

It Happens

It happens

On the mornings, when I wake up

It happens

When I go to fill my cup

It happens

When the pot isn't full

It happens

When life gets too dull

It happens

When I walk outdoors

It happens

When I do chores

It happens

When I see you

It happens

I wish you felt it too

Hunger

The caterpillars find leaves and eat as they
please,
they are no longer hungry.

The birds find worms and bees, they feast and
are at ease,
they are no longer hungry.

The snakes find birds and feast, their bellies full,
at peace,
they are no longer hungry.

The men scour the seas, they continue searching
at unease,
they remain hungry.

I Am So Sorry

I am so sorry,

I don't know what to do-

I shouldn't give up on you.

I am so sorry,

that I should have knew-

what would have happened if you grew?

I am so sorry,

        I gave up

  and

            let

   you

         wither.

Soiled

Someone crushed me on the ground and buried
me inside the earth.

My bones are aching letting out sound

 "Is this what I was worth?"

The spiders crawling all around

 stinging

 my

skin

their bites fueling my rebirth.

Outgrown

The grass in my mind shakes and my old back
aches
My warm indent has grown too small, to carry it
all.

The mud hardened and would not adjust
In new mud would I now have to trust.

Maybe in some years my hole would return to
dust
Then, maybe it would reform into a new crust.

It would be around my body once again,
embracing me as an old friend.

Stills And Sleeps

Silence stills and sleeps
and then
tucks me in my resting bed.

Silence tills and creeps
and then
enters into my lone head.

Silence drills and seeps
and then
I know it is the last time I'll close my eyes again.

The Rain

It is raining, and now

you
must
get
out
of
here.

I don't want the rain to show you what I fear.

For underneath all that muck is something that
must stay stuck, so please,

disappear.

I can't let you see her.

Parasite

Please kill the parasite inside me
I don't care what you do
If you need to drown it
That would be okay too
Just help me to feel less tired
Get me to walk again
If it died inside me then
And only then
I don't want to carry it around
I never asked for it
It didn't get permission to stay inside
Let me rip it out
I'll get my hands bloody
And tear my body apart
And to no avail will the parasite depart
I don't know what's better
Or I don't know what's worse
The pain of it inside me
Or the pain of cutting it out
Please just make it stop
I can't keep going like this

Where Misery Was Wrought

I was cooking a yummy meal, to fuel me and to
make me feel -
alive again, or so I thought-
I burnt myself, and became distraught.

My skin bright red with no appeal, I forgot about
my yummy meal!
I hated the fire, or so I thought-
and with it, I valiantly fought.

How could you burn me? I said with zeal.
With anger did my thoughts reel! But, as I
looked into my pot,
I started thinking about my lot.

Yes, the fire made me kneel, over with pain that
is real.
But I wanted to feel alive, and that is what I got,
through the fire where misery was wrought.

Tomato

A pretty tomato was given to me, and from it I
plucked a pretty seed

I was determined to make it grow, and so the
seed did I sow

I watered it with tender care, I gave it treatment I
thought fair

Months had passed when I saw a sprout, but
what I saw made me pout

A crooked stem and crumpled leaves, it seemed
to look very diseased!

But although it made me mad, I forgave it
because it made the most delicious tomatoes I
ever had.

Forest Changes

The forest around me changes

Once deeply rooted plants die as the wind rages

A fire comes in and decimates the life

The grassy floor is filled with continual strife

The gorgeous flowers wilt and rot

While the tall trees dry up and drop

Everything that was once good, destroyed like props

But, new growth starts to lop onto the forest floor

When everyone thought the forest was no more

The forest is still a forest, just different than before

The trees are still trees, and they will be forever more

The flowers bloom back, covering the past gore

So the forest comes back as though it never kept
score

of the past horrors it had to endure.

New Growth

Out in the woods there is a tree stump
The birds come and knock on it with big thumps
They peck and gnaw at it all day
Until the stump goes away
In its place, a hollow hole
A remnant showing the wilderness's toll
But a little sapling grows inside
Where only death was thought to reside

Even In The Night

Out in the garden, bright.
I'm sure you've seen it,
even in the night.

It is in the birds flight.
it shines down the darkest pit,
even in the night.

It will bring peace, and not fight.
It finds the loneliest bits,
even in the night.

It soars higher than any kite.
In one place it cannot sit,
out in the garden, bright.

 It's there even when the going is tight.
For it to stop would be unfit,
even in the night.

And even when you lose sight,
it is still there, lit.
Out in the garden, bright,
even in the night.

Evening

In the evening when I arose,

I heard small voices in gentle droves.

Calling out for me to see,

a world dressed in emerald, green.

I could hear its voice in the crows,

and in the small animal burrows.

I could hear it in the beans,

their stalks glistening clean.

I could hear it in the air,

damp mist covering me everywhere.

And so a gentle breeze did blow,

an eternal calm for my heart to stow.

Perfectly Made

You are like a huge tree, a wonderful sight for all to see.

I think what is best of all is you love me.

Sometimes, I think you hate me, because I can wield an axe.

Then you will remind me, those thoughts are not facts.

Your love cuts deeper than any manmade blade,

and reminds me I am perfectly made.

(:

Made New

I am so grateful
for what you do!
You took me,
and made me new!
I was worn out, disgusting,
and had nothing to do -
with something so wonderful, like you.

Hopecore

You took away my pain, and made me joyful
again.

I did not think it was true for someone to be able
to do

What you did for me, but now I see

With your perfect love, I am made happy.